The NuWave Oven Cookbook:
101 Delicious Nu-Wave Oven Recipes for the Countertop Connoisseur

by Lorraine Benedict

NMD
Books

NMD Books
Long Beach, CA

Copyright 2013 –Nu Wave Oven Cookbook

Library of Congress Cataloging-in-Publication Data

The NuWave Oven Cookbook:
101 Delicious Recipes for the Countertop
Connoisseur by Lorraine Benedict

ISBN: 978-1-936828-25-8   (Softcover)

First Edition April 2013

Table of Contents:

CASEROLES

COULD BE VEGETARIAN

MUFFINS

PASTRY - Savory

BREAKFAST

MUFFINS – Sweet

PIZZA

SNACKS

KIDS

NU WAVE TWISTER

BACON WRAPPED MEATLOAF

600g beef mince
1 cup breadcrumbs
½ cup spaghetti sauce
2 cloves garlic, minced
½ medium yellow onion, minced
1 tbsp dry Italian herbs
2 large eggs
¼ cup grated Parmesan cheese
200g thinly sliced bacon rashers (I use Thin 'n Crispy)
Piece of baking paper a little larger than the top of the loaf pan.

1. Spray loaf pan with oil and line pan with bacon rashers leaving extra length hanging over the sides of the pan.
2. Mix together the remaining ingredients.
3. Fill loaf pan with meat mixture and bring ends of bacon rashers into centre to seal.
4. Bake in **NuWave oven** on 2cm rack, level 10 for 20min.
5. Gently turn meatloaf over onto baking paper (on rack) and remove loaf pan. Cook for a further 30min.

Meatloaf is absolutely delicious hot and leftovers are wonderful served cold with salad or on sandwiches!

BEEF WELLINGTON

2 sheets ready made puff pastry
200g duxelles (very finely chopped mushrooms cooked
      down with onion & seasoning)
50g chicken or goose liver pate
4 equal portions of eye fillet steak 2.5cm thick

1. Cut the puff pastry in rounds large enough that when
   meat is placed in centre, the pastry is 2.5cm above the
   top of the meat when drawn up the sides. Cut another
   round large enough to cover the top of the meat.
2. In centre of each large circle of pastry gently spread
   one quarter of the pate and top with quarter of the
   mushroom duxelle. Place fillet on top of mushrooms,
   put small pastry round on top of meat.
3. Brush edges of pastry with egg white, draw pastry up
   and join to top round – ensure you have a good seal.
4. Bake in **NuWave oven** on 10cm rack (sprayed with
   oil) for 10 minutes, turn over and bake for a further 5
   minutes or until golden. For well done (no pink) place
   on 5cm rack and cook for a total of 20 minutes.

Mushroom Duxelle

*For basic duxelles, mince 250g fresh mushrooms (or mushroom stems)
and 1 small onion or 1 to 2 shallots. In a frying pan, sauté the onion or
shallot in 1 to 2 tablespoons butter until soft but not brown (3 to 5
minutes). Stir in minced mushrooms, salt and pepper, chopped parsley
to taste, and a pinch of tarragon or thyme if you wish. Depending on
your main course, any fresh herb(s) or splash of soy sauce, white wine,
Madeira, lemon juice, or even fruit, such as dried apricots, can be
added. Cook the mixture over medium high heat until the mushrooms
give off a lot of liquid; that liquid will evaporate completely (5 to 10
minutes). The duxelles will look like a coarse mash. Cool the mixture
slightly and taste for seasoning. This will make about 1-1/2 cups.
Duxelles may be frozen for 1 to 2 months.*

   This is an impressive main course and is easily mastered! Enjoy!

CORNED BEEF

1kg - 1½kg corned silverside (salt reduced)
1 cup beef stock
10 peppercorns
6 whole cloves (or 1/8 tsp ground cloves)
1 bayleaf

1. Rinse off the meat and place everything in plastic cooking bag.** Lay on 2cm (1") rack.
2. Cook in **NuWave oven**, power level HI for 1½hrs. Carefully turn bag over and cook an additional 45-60min or until meat is tender.

Note: Making slits in the cooking bag will result in juices escaping from the bag. Instead gather the open end of the bag, leave a thumb size opening and tie with string or ties.

This is most fuss-free and delicious way to cook silverside! When you turn the bag over pile vegetables on rack around bag such as potatoes, sweet potatoes, pumpkin and carrots and cook at the same time! In fact, transfer to 5cm rack when turning bag and place an alfoil pack of shredded cabbage (a sprinkling of water and a knob of butter added) underneath as well and you have a complete meal!

EASY COTTAGE PIE

750g beef mince
1 pkt French onion soup mix
½ cup water
2 cups frozen peas & corn (or 1 cup peas & corn + 1 cup mixed veg)
1 tbsp Worcestershire sauce
1 tbsp tomato sauce
1 tsp soy sauce
1 tbsp plain flour (mixed to a loose paste with a little water)

Topping
3 – 4 cups mashed potato
OR
2 cups mashed potato and
2 cups mashed kumara

1. Brown mince in fry pan, add soup mix and water. Stir.
2. Simmer on low heat until meat is tender (add a little more water if necessary).
3. Add remaining ingredients, and stir until thick.
4. Pour into pan (the one that comes with the extender kit) or shallow casserole dish.
5. Top with mashed potato and dot with butter. If using both potato and kumara try piping alternate stripes – looks great.
6. Bake in **NuWave oven** on 5cm rack, level 10 for 25 mins or until golden brown.

This is a complete meal in itself and the kids (big ones too!) will love it! You can also replace the mince with any leftover roast meat – a tasty way to use up the leftovers.

SAUSAGE PITA ROLLS

5 large pita bread
10 thin sausages

Cold filling
1 small lettuce, shredded
150g alfalfa sprouts
2 large carrots, grated
2 cups grated cheddar cheese
3 large tomatoes, seeded & sliced into strips

Dressing
250ml bottle Thousand Island dressing
2 tbsp mayonnaise
1 tsp French mustard
2 shallots, chopped

1. Split each pita bread into two rounds.
2. Bake sausages in **NuWave oven**, 10cm rack, for 10 min (fresh) or 15 min (frozen).
3. Place a hot sausage on each pita round.
4. Sprinkle with grated carrot, tomato strips, shredded lettuce, sprouts and grated cheese.
5. Spoon on dressing, roll up pita bread.

Dressing
Combine Thousand Island dressing, mayonnaise, mustard and shallots.

An easy, fat free, healthier way to satisfy hungry kids – both big and small!

SAUSAGES WITH PRUNES & BACON

4 thick sausages
12 pitted prunes
2 rashers bacon

1. With a sharp knife, gently make a slit in each sausage being careful not to cut right through.
2. Into each sausage, stuff 3 prunes into slit.
3. Cut each bacon rasher into 2 lengthways and diagonally wrap around sausage and fix with a cocktail stick.
4. Bake in **NuWave oven** on 10cm rack, level 10 for 15 minutes, turning sausages after 10 minutes.

A fun, different and delicious way to serve an old family favourite!

LAMB & ROSEMARY COTTAGE PIE

800g potatoes, peeled and chopped
1 tbsp butter
¼ cup milk
1 tbsp oil
1 onion, finely diced
2 cloves garlic, chopped
500g lamb mince
2 carrots, grated
2 tbsp tomato paste
1 teasp dried rosemary
2 tbsp plain flour
1½ cups beef stock
½ cup grated tasty cheese

1. Place potatoes in saucepan of boiling salted water. Cook for 20 minutes or until tender. Drain, return to saucepan, add butter & milk, mash until smooth.
2. Heat oil in a saucepan over medium heat. Add onions & garlic, cook for 5mins until softened. Add mince & carrot, cook until browned.
3. Add tomato paste & rosemary, cook stirring for 2mins. Remove from heat.
4. Stir in flour. Slowly add stock, stirring after each addition, until combined. Return to heat. Cook for a further 5mins, stirring constantly, until sauce has thickened. Spoon into a 23cm pie dish.
5. Top with mashed potato, then sprinkle over cheese.
6. Bake in **NuWave oven**, on 10cm rack, for 10-15mins or until golden.

PASTICCIO

40g butter
2 tbsp plain flour
1½ cups milk
1 cup parmesan cheese, finely grated
250g dried penne pasta

Meat Sauce
1 tbsp olive oil
1 med brown onion, finely chopped
3 cloves garlic, crushed
2 tbsp tomato paste
500g lamb mince
400g can diced tomatoes
1 cinnamon stick
½ cup fresh flat-leaf parsley leaves

Make meat sauce
1. Heat oil in a large saucepan over high heat. Add onion and garlic. Cook, stirring, for 3-4 minutes or until onion has softened.
2. Add tomato paste. Cook, stirring, for one minute.
3. Add mince. Cook, stirring with a wooden spoon to break up mince, for 6-8 minutes or until browned.
4. Add tomato and cinnamon. Season with salt and pepper. Bring to the boil. Reduce heat to low and simmer for 20-35 minutes or until sauce has thickened. Remove from heat.
5. Remove and discard cinnamon stick. Stir in parsley.

1. Melt butter in a saucepan over medium-high heat. Add flour. Cook, stirring, for one minute or until bubbling.
2. Gradually stir in milk. Bring to the boil. Reduce heat to medium. Cook, stirring, for 5 minutes or until mixture has thickened. Remove from heat. Stir in half the cheese. Season with salt and pepper.
3. Cook pasta in a large saucepan of boiling, salted water, following packet directions until tender. Drain.

4. Add pasta to meat sauce. Stir to combine.
5. Spoon into 25cm ovenproof dish (the one that comes with the extender kit is perfect). Top with cheese sauce. Sprinkle with remaining cheese.
6. Bake in **NuWave oven** on 5cm rack, level 10 for 20 minutes or until golden.

Serve with a crisp green salad.

HONEY PORK/CHICKEN WRAPS

1 sheet puff pastry (thawed)
500g pork or chicken fillets (cut into strips)
1 tsp Chinese five spice
½ tbsp soy sauce
½ tbsp honey
½ cup julienne cut carrots
½ cup julienne cut zucchini
½ cup julienne cut red capsicum
1 lightly beaten egg (for glazing pastry)

1. Combine pork or chicken with Chinese five-spice, soy sauce and honey in a bowl.
2. Pour mixture into frying pan and lightly stir-fry until meat is just cooked.
3. Cut pastry into 4 squares.
4. Divide meat and vegetables down the diagonal centre of each pastry square and fold corners over filling.
5. Glaze top with beaten egg.
6. Place on 10cm rack and bake in **NuWave oven** for 10 minutes turning over for last 2 minutes.

Fabulous for an entrée, kid's snack or light luncheon!

FILLET OF PORK with CHILI MANGO COULIS

1 pork fillet
Fresh ground salt
Coulis

1tbsp sweet chili sauce
1 fresh mango
1 small red chili, sliced & de-seeded
1. Place pork fillet on 10cm rack of **NuWave oven** and bake on HI for 20mins, turning halfway.
2. In **NuWave Twister** place mango, chili sauce and chili. Pulsate until pulped and combined.
3. Serve warm pork slices with coulis and a fresh salad.

Amazingly quick to prepare, healthy and delicious!

ROAST PORK

1 roasting joint of pork (leg, loin,)
1 tbsp oil
Cooking salt

1. Weigh pork to calculate cooking time.
2. Score rind of pork about 1 cm apart – (ask butcher to do this for you).
3. Massage oil into skin of pork and into cuts.
4. Generously sprinkle salt over skin (approx 1 tbsp salt)
5. Bake in **NuWave oven** on 2cm rack, level 10 for 25mins per ½kg.

Nothing puts the crunch into pork crackling like the NuWave oven!!

TANDOORI PORK BELLY

1 kg piece of boneless pork belly, rind on
2 tsp salt
¼ cup tandoori curry paste
1 cup chicken stock, heated

1. Score the rind on the pork belly in a crisscross fashion 1cm apart. It's easier to ask your butcher to do this!
2. Rub salt well into skin.
3. Cut piece into four.
4. Coat other three sides of pork generously with curry paste.
5. Stand skin side up in pan (I use the one that comes with the extender kit – it's perfect) and gently pour in chicken stock at side (don't wet the rind!)
6. Bake in **NuWave oven** on 5cm rack, level 10 for 50-60 mins or until pork is tender.

Serve with rice and a crisp garden salad and crunchy bread.

CHICKEN, ALMOND & BACON FILLED CROISSANTS

4 Croissants
¼ chicken, cooked (barbequed is perfect)
2 rashers bacon, chopped
2 tbsp slivered almonds
1 tbsp chopped chives
½ cup sour cream

1. Toast almonds* in **NuWave oven**, 10cm rack for 4 minutes.
2. Remove chicken meat from bones and chop chicken finely.
3. Cook bacon in pan until crisp and drain.
4. Combine chicken, bacon, almonds, chives and sour cream.
5. Fill croissants with mixture and bake in **NuWave oven** on 10cm rack for 8 minutes, turning after 5mins.

I use the pan that comes with the extender kit for toasting the nuts – it's perfect!

These are just the answer for a brunch, a stunning light lunch served with salad, a late supper or a great solution for people on the go! Don't stop here – try other fillings like sautéed mushrooms & bacon, sweet corn & chicken, cream cheese, chives & lemon or make up your own combination.

CHICKEN, CHEESE & SPINACH PASTA BAKE

½ cooked chicken*
200g pasta (penne, tortiglioni or rigatoni work well)
½ tbsp olive oil
1 clove garlic
1/2 small red onion
250g jar tomato pasta sauce
1 cup tasty or pizza cheese
50g baby spinach leaves
Pepper & Salt to taste

1. Cook pasta in a large saucepan of boiling salted water until just tender. Drain and return to saucepan.
2. Meanwhile, heat oil in a frypan over medium to high heat. Add garlic and onion, cook, stirring often until onion is tender and transparent (around 4 minutes).
3. Add onion mixture, pasta sauce, chopped chicken meat, half of the cheese and spinach to hot pasta. Season with salt and pepper. Toss gently until well combined.
4. Spoon pasta mixture into a greased pan (I use the dish that comes with the extender kit but a cake pan or casserole dish is fine). Sprinkle top with remaining cheese.
5. Bake in **NuWave oven**, on 5cm rack for 15mins.

*Barbeque chicken can be used for this recipe, however you can cook a chicken or 2 chicken breasts in your **NuWave oven** just as easily and this is more cost efficient!*

CHICKEN, CORN & CHEESE ENCHILADAS

½ tbsp olive oil
½ onion, finely chopped
1 clove garlic
½ tsp paprika
200g chicken mince
160g can creamed corn
½ cup frozen corn kernels
¼ cup chopped fresh parsley
½ cup grated tasty cheese
4 flour tortillas
190g jar tomato & capsicum enchilada simmer sauce (or half of a 375g jar)

1. Heat oil in a non-stick frypan. Add onion, garlic and paprika. Cook, stirring occasionally, until onion is soft.
2. Add chicken. Cook, stirring, until chicken has changed colour.
3. Add creamed corn and kernels.
4. Bring to boil. Simmer, stirring occasionally, for about 5 minutes, or until slightly thickened.
5. Stir in parsley and half of the cheese.
6. Divide chicken mixture among tortillas and roll up to enclose filling.
7. Spread a third of the simmer sauce over base of 25cm pan (extender dish is perfect for this). Arrange tortillas side by side over sauce. Pour remaining sauce over top and sprinkle with remaining cheese.
8. Bake in **NuWave oven** on 5cm rack, level 10 for 20mins.

Serve with sour cream and a crisp garden salad.

This is so tasty – all the family will love it! Double the recipe to make more!

CHICKEN, SPINACH & CHEESE GNOCCHI

1 300ml tub thin cream
1 chicken breast, chopped
1 clove garlic
1 packet (400-500g) potato gnocchi
¼ cup grated parmesan
100g shaved ham, thinly sliced
100g baby spinach leaves
salt & pepper, to taste
½ cup grated pizza cheese (a mixture of mozzarella, parmesan & tasty cheese)

1. Place cream and chicken in a large saucepan. Bring to the boil and simmer for 5 minutes. Remove from heat and set aside.
2. Add gnocchi to a large saucepan of boiling, salted water. Boil gently for about 3 minutes, or until gnocchi rises to the surface. Drain.
3. Add gnocchi, parmesan, ham and spinach to chicken mixture. Season with salt and pepper. Stir well.
4. Divide mixture evenly among four ovenproof dishes (1¼ cup capacity). Sprinkle with pizza cheese.
5. Bake in **NuWave oven** on 5cm rack, level 10 for 15mins.

Serve with crisp garden salad.

CHICKEN PARMESAN

4 x 180g boneless/skinless chicken breasts – FROZEN
Italian dressing
Seasoned bread crumbs
250g grated pizza cheese
Grated parmesan to taste
½ cup pasta sauce

1. Combine seasoned breadcrumbs with grated parmesan.
2. Dip chicken pieces in Italian dressing and roll in bread crumbs.
3. Place on 10cm rack and NuWave 13mins per side (or until done).
4. Open oven and spoon sauce on each piece and sprinkle with cheese.
5. NuWave for 2-3 minutes until cheese is golden.
6. Remove chicken from oven and allow chicken to rest for about 5-10 minutes before cutting.

For a low-cal version try using low-fat Italian dressing and light mozzarella in place of the pizza cheese – both versions will delight!

CRUNCHY CHEESE FILLED CHICKEN

Ingredients
4 boneless chicken breasts
90g cheddar cheese
1 tbsp Dijon mustard
1 cup crushed corn flakes
1 tsp dried parsley flakes
½ cup buttermilk

Method
1. Cut a deep 5cm long slit in the side of the meaty portion of the breast.
2. Slice cheese into 4 portions and brush with mustard. Place 1 piece of cheese into each slit and secure with wooden toothpicks.
3. Combine cereal, seasoning and parsley.
4. Dip chicken into buttermilk and roll in cereal mixture.
5. Place chicken on baking paper on 10cm rack and bake in **NuWave oven** on power level HI for 30 minutes, turn over ½ way thru to evenly brown.

Replace cheese with low fat, and buttermilk with non fat, for a healthier option of this recipe!

TURKEY & APPLE MEATLOAVES

500g turkey mince
1 egg, lightly beaten
1 apple, peeled and grated
1 onion, finely chopped
2 slices bread, diced
2 tsp olive oil

1. Grease 6 mini-rectangle oven dishes.
2. Mix together turkey mince, grated apple, onion and egg until combined.
3. Divide mixture equally between baking dishes. Smooth tops.
4. In a small bowl toss diced bread with olive oil. Spoon the oiled bread on top of each mini meatloaf.
5. Bake in **NuWave oven** on 5cm rack, level 10 for 15-20mins or until cooked through.

Served with a salad and you have a perfect lunch or dinner!

BAKED LOBSTER TAIL WITH BACON MORNAY

1 lobster tail, meat removed and roughly chopped
2 bacon rashers, finely chopped
40g butter
1½ tbsp plain flour
1½ cups milk
1 egg yolk
2 tbsp flat leaf parsley, chopped
Lemon wedges to serve

1. Heat oil in a frying pan over medium heat, add the lobster and bacon and cook for 4-5 minutes or until lobster is golden and bacon is crispy.
2. Melt butter in a small saucepan over medium heat until foaming. Add flour, cook, stirring, for 1 minute or until bubbling.
3. Remove from heat and slowly add milk, whisking continuously, until mixture is smooth.
4. Return to heat reducing heat to low. Cook, stirring with a wooden spoon, for 3-5 minutes or until sauce comes to the boil. Remove from heat and whisk in egg yolk and season with salt and pepper.
5. Place lobster in a shallow pan (extender kit pan is ideal) and pour sauce over. Top with bacon.
6. Bake in **NuWave oven** on 10cm rack, level 10 for 5mins or top is golden.
7. Sprinkle with parsley and serve with lemon wedges.

An absolutely delicious dish to serve for that special occasion!

CREAMY TUNA MORNAY

30g butter
1 medium brown onion (finely chopped)
1 trimmed stick celery (chopped finely)
1 tbsp plain flour
¾ cup milk
½ cup cream
⅓ cup grated cheddar cheese
130g can corn kernels, drained
185g can tuna, drained
½ cup stale breadcrumbs
¼ cup grated cheddar, extra

1. Melt butter in a frypan on a moderate heat and add onion.
2. Cook for about 3 minutes, add celery and cook another 2 minutes or until celery softens.
3. Add flour to pan and cook for 1 or 2 minutes.
4. Remove pan from heat and gradually add milk and cream, stirring constantly.
5. Return to heat, stirring until mixture boils and thickens.
6. Add cheese, stirring until cheese is melted.
7. Gently fold in corn and tuna.
8. Divide mixture evenly into 2 individual casserole dishes (2 cup capacity).
9. Sprinkle combined breadcrumbs and extra cheese over top.
10. Bake in **NuWave oven** on 5cm rack, level 10 for 12 – 15 minutes or golden brown and crispy on top.

This recipe serves two. Simply double up to serve four! Creamy Tuna Mornays are a tasty meal with ingredients easily found in the cupboard and fridge and still bursting with nutritional value.

CURRIED PRAWNS

750g green prawns (shelled)
60g butter
1 tbsp curry powder
2 sticks celery, chopped
1 large onion, finely diced
½ green pepper
1 medium tomato, peeled and diced
4 tbsp plain flour
Pepper & Salt to taste
1½ cups water
1 cup milk
2 tsp chicken stock powder
1 tsp sugar
1 tbsp lemon juice

1. In frypan melt butter, add curry powder, celery, onion and pepper. Cook gently, stirring 2-3min.
2. Add tomato to pan and cook a further 2min.
3. Stir in flour, pepper and salt and cook, stirring for one minute.
4. Remove from heat, and gradually add water and milk. Add stock powder and return to heat. Cook, stirring, until sauce boils and thickens.
5. Transfer sauce to ovenproof shallow dish (the dish that comes with the extender kit is perfect)
6. Bake in **NuWave oven**, on 10cm rack for 10mins.
7. Add prawns, stir and bake a further 10mins.
8. Serve with plenty of steamed rice and enjoy!

Try pre-cooking your rice and using an ovenproof container (foil over the top) and place it on the liner tray to heat through/keep hot while the curry cooks!

FILO WRAPPED SALMON WITH GREEK YOGURT & DILL DRESSING

1 Salmon fillet
3 sheets filo pastry (which has been sprayed with canola oil)
Large dollop of Greek yoghurt with fresh dill added

1. Wrap salmon in the filo to make a parcel.
2. Bake in **NuWave oven** on 10cm rack, level 10 for 8mins; turn and brown other side for about 4mins.
3. Serve with dollop of Greek yoghurt with dill and hot chips (can be cooked at the same time)

FRESH SALMON PIE

300g fresh skinless salmon portions
1 tbsp olive oil
½ med onion, finely chopped
50g small mushrooms, finely slices
¼ cup long grain cooked rice, cooled
1 tsp fresh dill, chopped
1 tbsp thin cream
2 hardboiled eggs, chopped
2 sheets frozen puff pastry, thawed
1 extra egg, beaten

1. Wrap salmon in baking paper and bake in **NuWave oven** for 10-15 min (depending on thickness), on 10cm rack. Unwrap and allow to cool.
2. Heat oil in frypan; cook onions on med heat for 5mins, until soft.
3. Add mushrooms and cook further 2mins, until soft.
4. Transfer mixture to large mixing bowl and cool slightly.
5. Add rice, dill, cream and eggs, season with salt & pepper, mix well.
6. Lay out 1 sheet of pastry on baking paper and spread rice mixture down centre of pastry allowing 5cm at each end and 10cm either side.
7. Break salmon into chunks and place on top of rice.
8. Top with other sheet of pastry and gently mould it around the filling.
9. Cut sides to even them and fold all edges over toward center, pressing to seal.
10. Gently cut diagonal slits in top pastry and brush with extra egg.
11. Cook bottom side up, in **NuWave oven** on 5cm rack, for 10mins. Turn and cook a further 20 minutes.

GARLIC PRAWN ROLLS

6 small par-baked French bread rolls
75g unsalted butter
2 cloves garlic, crushed
1 tbsp flat leaf parsley, chopped
½ kg cooked & peeled small prawns *(green prawns can be used – see note below)*

1. Make cut lengthways in the top of each bread roll.
2. Melt butter with garlic together, stirring, in a small pan.*
3. Remove from heat and use a pastry brush to brush the insides of the rolls with some of the garlic butter.
4. Add parsley to garlic butter and then stir in prawns.
5. Fill each roll with the prawn mixture and place on 10cm rack.
6. Bake in **NuWave oven** for 5-6mins.

Serve hot.
* *If using green prawns, add them to the melted garlic butter and cook, stirring until just done.*

This is a scrumptious dish just perfect for a snack with drinks, a quick and easy lunch with salad or an entrée that will be a big hit!

KIM'S SOY SALMON

2 fresh salmon fillets, about 2½ cm thick
1 tbsp ketjap manis (a sweet Indonesian soy sauce
            available from the Asian section of your
            supermarket)
1 tbsp soy sauce
2 tbsp sweet chili sauce
1 tbsp fresh ginger, finely grated 1tbsp lemon or lime
juice

1. Mix together ketjap manis, soy sauce, sweet chili
   sauce, grated ginger and lemon or lime juice.
2. Coat salmon fillets with sauce mixture and place in
   NuWave oven on baking paper on 10cm rack.
3. Bake in **NuWave oven**, 15 mins or until cooked
   through (this will depend on the thickness of the
   salmon).

MOROCCAN FISH SKEWERS

Ingredients
8 pre-soaked bamboo skewers
600g ling fillets, cubed
Moroccan Spice Rub
2 tsp lemon pepper
1 tsp paprika
½ tsp ground turmeric
½ tsp ground coriander

Method
Make Moroccan spice rub:
1. Combine lemon pepper, paprika, turmeric and coriander in a glass or ceramic bowl.
2. Add fish, toss to coat. Cover. Refrigerate for 1 or 2 hours, if time permits.
3. Thread fish onto skewers.
4. Bake in **NuWave oven** on 10cm rack, power level HI, for 6-8 minutes or just cooked through (do not over cook).

A healthy delight with a crisp garden salad!

LINDY'S SALMON FLORENTINE

4 Atlantic Salmon fillets (or less if you like a thicker topping)
I cup baby spinach leaves, (tightly packed down)
1 cup fresh breadcrumbs
2/3 cup finely grated Parmesan cheese
1 clove garlic, finely chopped / or 1 tsp minced garlic
Drizzle of olive oil
Salt and pepper

1. After processing fresh bread (approx 6 slices, crusts off) into fine crumbs using a food processor, add the spinach leaves and pulse till combined and chopped into the crumbs, add in most of the parmesan cheese and a drizzle of olive oil, garlic and salt and pepper and pulse briefly until all combined. The mixture will be a thick pasty consistency.
2. Spread a thick layer of this onto the top of each salmon fillet (serving side up) and sprinkle a little extra of the grated cheese you reserved on top.
3. On the 10cm rack sprayed with olive oil to ensure no sticking (or the 5cm that comes with the extender kit if you prefer a lighter colour result, ie further from heat source) add the salmon Florentine topped fillets.
4. In **NuWave oven** at high power setting (no. 10) bake the fillets for 12-14 minutes depending on thickness. No need to turn during cook time.
5. Serve with a green salad and garlic bread rolls (made in the **NuWave** of course!)

Thanks Lindy for this fantastic recipe! A true winner!!

NUTTY ORANGE CHILI SALMON

2 Salmon fillets
2 tbsp orange marmalade
1½ tsp hot chili flakes
75g dry roasted chopped cashews, peanuts, almonds &
    pistachios (leave whole)*

1. Combine marmalade, chili flakes and nuts in a bowl. Mix well.
2. Pack half mixture on skinless side of each salmon fillet.
3. Bake in **NuWave oven** on 10cm rack, level 10 for 12 mins or salmon is cooked through to your liking.

This mixture of nuts is available in good supermarkets.

An easy and quick, yet delightfully unique and delicious way to cook salmon! Enjoy!

THAI CHILI SNAPPER

1 snapper, whole with head removed (around 800g)
4 cloves garlic, crushed
¼ cup finely chopped fresh lemongrass
¼ cup chopped fresh coriander
2 fresh small red Thai chilies, chopped finely
2 tbsp mild sweet chili sauce
4cm piece fresh ginger, finely grated
1 tbsp Thai red curry paste
2 tbsp lime juice

1. Combine all ingredients except fish in a medium bowl.
2. Cut four shallow slits in each side of fish, making sure you don't cut through bones.
3. Coat both sides of fish with chili mix and allow to marinate in fridge for 3 hours or overnight.
4. Pulling flaps of fish out, stand fish upright on 5cm rack.
5. Bake in **NuWave oven** for 20-25mins.

Fantastic!

TACO CHICKEN STRIPS

400g chicken tenderloins
35g pkt mild taco seasoning mix
1 cup light sour cream
200g plain corn chips, crushed

1. Place seasoning mix and sour cream in a shallow bowl. Stir to combine. Place chips on a plate.
2. Dip 1 piece chicken into seasoning mixture. Coat in chips.
3. Refrigerate for 30 minutes.
4. Spray chicken with spray oil and place on 10cm rack.
5. Bake in **NuWave oven** for 12 minutes turning over for last couple of minutes.
6. Serve with lemon wedges.

A fun way to serve chicken and it goes great with an avocado salsa!

TUNA & SWEETCORN POTATOES

4 large potatoes (1.5kg)
25g butter
1 onion, finely chopped
1 clove garlic
185g can tuna, drained
310g can sweet corn kernels, drained
1/3 cup sour cream
¼ cup chopped fresh chives
1 cup grated tasty cheese
salt & pepper, to taste

1. Wash unpeeled potatoes well and pierce all over with a fork. Cook in **NuWave oven** for 40 minutes or until tender.
2. Melt butter in frypan, add onion and garlic. Cook, stirring, for 2 minutes.
3. Cut potatoes in half (lengthways) and carefully scoop out flesh, leaving a 1cm thick shell. Place flesh in large bowl and mash with a fork.
4. Add tuna mixture, sour cream, chives and ½ cup of the cheese. Season with salt & pepper. Mix well.
5. Spoon filling back into potato half shells and sprinkle with remaining cheese.
6. Bake in **NuWave oven** on 5cm rack, level 10 for 15 minutes or until cheese has melted and golden brown.

Serve with crisp garden salad.

Makes a delicious lunch or dinner! For weight-watchers simply replace the sour cream with light sour cream.

CHICKEN & WHITE WINE CASSEROLE

500g chicken thigh fillets (cut into about 5 pieces each)
2 tbsp olive oil
2-3 cloves garlic (crushed)
3 rashers bacon (cut into pieces)
2 red capsicums
400g canned diced tomatoes
¼ cup white wine
2 lge sprigs fresh thyme

1. Heat oil in frypan on moderately high heat, add and brown chicken pieces. Remove from pan.
2. Add garlic, bacon and capsicum to pan and cook until capsicum is soft and bacon browned.
3. Add tomatoes, wine and thyme sprigs. Stir.
4. Place chicken pieces into 24cm round shallow dish (I use the pan that came with my extender kit – it's perfect!).
5. Pour over bacon mixture and place into **NuWave oven** on 5cm rack.
6. Cook in **NuWave** (level 10), 10cm rack for 45 minutes.

Bon Appetite!

BAKED STUFFED EGGPLANT

1 medium eggplant 2 medium tomatoes, peeled, chopped
Course cooking salt ¾ cup cooked brown rice
1 tbsp oil 1 tbsp fresh chives, chopped
1 small onion, finely chopped ½ cup grated tasty cheese
1 clove garlic, crushed 2 tbsp grated parmesan cheese
2 rashers bacon or ham, chopped

1. Slice eggplant in half lengthways, scoop out flesh,
   leaving 2cm shell; sprinkle inside shells and scooped
   flesh with salt; stand 30min. Rinse under water to
   remove salt; drain on absorbent paper
2. Chop flesh roughly.
3. Heat oil in saucepan, add onion, garlic and bacon,
   cook, stirring, for about 5min or until soft.
4. Add tomatoes and flesh, cover, cook over heat for
   about 2min or until soft.
5. Add ¼ cup of the rice, mix well, spoon into eggplant.
6. Combine remaining rice, chives and cheeses in a small
   bowl, sprinkle evenly over eggplant.
7. Place on 5cm rack, wrap loosely with baking paper and
   bake in **NuWave oven** level 10 for 20mins removing
   paper for last 10mins.

*A fabulous tasty way to serve eggplant! Replace the ham with another
vegetable for a delicious vegetarian dish!*

BEAN CASSEROLE WITH POTATO SCONES

CASSEROLE
420g can 4 bean mix, drained
1 tsp vegetable oil
1 small onion sliced
¼ cup vegetable stock
1 teasp Cajun or Moroccan seasoning
½ teasp cumin
½ red capsicum, chopped
½ yellow capsicum, chopped
1 finger eggplant, sliced
1 small zucchini, sliced
125g fresh asparagus, chopped
75g fresh beans, chopped
½ cup frozen corn kernels
3 medium tomatoes, peeled & chopped

POTATO SCONES *You will need to cook about 2 large potatoes (600g) for this recipe*
1½ cups self-raising flour
60g butter, chopped
1 tbsp fresh basil, chopped
¼ cup grated tasty cheddar cheese
1¼ cups cooked potato, mashed
¼ cup milk, approximately

CASSEROLE
—. Heat oil in flameproof casserole dish (1.5ltr capacity)*, add onion, cook, stirring, until onion is soft.
—. Add beans, stock, spices and vegetables and simmer for 5 minutes.
—. Top with scones, brush lightly with egg wash or a little milk and bake in **NuWave oven** on 2cm rack for 20 minutes or until scones are golden brown.

POTATO SCONES

—. Sift flour into bowl, rub in butter until mixture
   resembles breadcrumbs.
—. Stir in basil, cheese, potato and enough milk to mix to
   a soft dough.
—. Turn dough onto a lightly floured surface and knead
   until smooth.
—. Roll or pat dough to 1.2cm thickness, cut into 4cm-5cm
   rounds.
—.

CRUSTLESS QUICHE - BACON & MUSHROOM

6 rashers of rindless bacon, diced
1tbsp oil
1 medium onion, finely diced
350g button mushrooms, halved
6 eggs, lightly whisked
½ cup milk
2/3 cup sour cream
1 cup grated cheddar cheese
1½ cups stale white coarse breadcrumbs (this will take
        about 2 slices of toast thick bread for food
        processor)
40g butter, melted

1. Using the 23cm pan that comes with the **NuWave oven extender kit**, add bacon and cook on 10cm rack in **NuWave oven** for 8min until crisp.
2. Add onion and mushrooms to pan, stir well and cook a further 3mins.
3. Transfer mushroom mixture to base of greased 26cm pie dish.
4. In medium bowl whisk eggs, sour cream, milk and cheese; pour over bacon mixture.
5. Combine breadcrumbs and butter in a small bowl: sprinkle over egg mixture.
6. Cook on 5cm rack in **NuWave oven** for 30-40mins. Pie will puff up and pull slightly away from the sides when cooked.
7. Allow to stand for 10 minutes before serving.

A fantastic quiche with a crunchy topping that cooks beautifully in the NuWave oven and is perfect served with a salad for any time of the day or night!

STUFFED CAPSICUMS

2 green capsicums
1 tbsp oil
30g butter
½ small onion, finely chopped
¼ cup celery, finely chopped
250g minced meat
½ cup cooked rice
¼ tsp chili flakes
¼ tsp paprika
1 tsp dried Italian herbs
1 tbsp tomato salsa
¼ cup parmesan cheese

1. Cut capsicums lengthways; remove seeds and membranes. Place capsicums in boiling water with oil and boil for 3 minutes. Drain well. Season inside of capsicums with salt and pepper.
2. Heat butter, add onion and celery, sauté until tender; add meat, rice, chili, paprika and herbs.
3. Cook, stirring constantly, until meat changes colour. Stir in salsa.
4. Place meat mixture into capsicum halves and top with parmesan cheese.
5. Bake in **NuWave oven** on 5cm rack for 15-20mins (depending on size of capsicums).

An oldie but a goodie – your recipe for the filling can be used also!

MACARONI CHEESE WITH VEGETABLES

50g butter, chopped
2 tbsp plain flour
2 cups milk
1 tsp Dijon mustard
½ cup parmesan cheese, grated
1¼ cups gouda cheese, grated
300g macaroni pasta, dried
1 large carrot
300g broccoli, cut into small florets
280g cauliflower, cut into small florets
4 shallots, thinly sliced

1. Melt butter in a saucepan over medium heat for 2 minutes or until foaming.
2. Add flour. Cook, stirring with a wooden spoon, for about 1 minute until mixture bubbles.
3. Remove from heat. Add milk, ¼ cup at a time, stirring constantly to prevent lumps forming.
4. Return pan to medium heat. Cook, stirring, for 5 minutes or until sauce boils and thickens. Remove from heat.
5. Stir in mustard, parmesan and 1 cup of the gouda cheese.
6. Meanwhile, cook pasta in a large saucepan of boiling water, following packet directions, adding the carrot, broccoli and cauliflower in the last 5 minutes of cooking. Drain. Place in a large bowl.
7. Add sauce and onion. Stir to combine. Spoon into 25cm dish (the one that comes with the extender kit is perfect).
8. Bake in **NuWave oven** on 5cm rack, level 10, for about 20 minutes, until hot through and golden brown.
9. Stand for 5 minutes before serving.

A delicious healthier alternative for that ever popular dish of macaroni cheese!

NUWAVE STYLE MUSHROOMS

12 large closed cup mushrooms
¼ cup ricotta cheese
½ cup fresh spinach
2 tbsp parmesan cheese, grated
1 garlic clove
½ small onion
2 tbsp vegetable stock

1. Pop the stems out of the mushrooms and wipe them clean
2. Place all the remaining ingredients in the short cup of **NuWave Twister** and fit the cross blade. Pulse until almost smooth. Spoon mixture into the mushrooms.
3. Bake in **NuWave oven** on 10cm rack, level 10 for 15mins.

A colourful and delicious way to serve mushrooms on their own or as a side dish.

STUFFED MUSHROOMS

2 large field mushrooms
1 tbsp oil
15g butter
½ tsp plain flour
1/8 tsp French mustard
2 tbsp milk
1 tbsp tasty cheese, grated
½ cup frozen mixed vegetables
½ tbsp flat leaf parsley, chopped
grated tasty cheese, extra
pepper & salt to taste

1. Remove centre core of mushrooms and discard. Rub outer side of mushrooms with the oil.
2. Make a thick cheese sauce by melting butter in a small saucepan, add flour and stir over heat for 1 minute.
3. Remove from heat and gradually add the milk and mustard. Return to heat and stir constantly until thick (feel free to add a touch more milk if necessary but remember that it is meant to be quite thick).
4. Stir in cheese until melted.
5. Add the mixed vegetables and parsley.
6. Fill mushrooms with the vegetable mixture and top with extra cheese
7. Bake in **NuWave oven** on 10cm rack for 8-10mins.

A great way to serve vegetables!

CHEESE, CORN & BACON MUFFINS

½ cup polenta *Cornmeal*
½ cup milk
3 rashers bacon, rindless and chopped finely
4 shallots, chopped finely
1½ cups self raising flour
1 tbsp caster sugar *Very fine sugar*
310g can corn kernels, drained
125g can creamed corn
100g butter, melted
2 eggs, beaten lightly
50g piece cheddar cheese
¼ cup coarsely grated cheddar cheese

1. Mix polenta and milk in small bowl; cover, stand 20 minutes.
2. Meanwhile, cook bacon, stirring, in heated small non-stick frying pan for 2 minutes. Add shallots and cook, stirring, for another 2 minutes. Remove pan from heat; cool bacon mixture about 5 minutes.
3. Sift flour and sugar into large bowl; stir in corn kernels, creamed corn and bacon mixture. Add melted butter, egg and polenta mixture; mix muffin batter only until just combined.
4. Spoon 1 tablespoon of the batter into each hole of the muffin pan. Cut the piece of cheese into 12 equal pieces, about the size of a 3cm cube; place one piece in the middle of the batter in muffin pan hole. Cover with remaining batter and sprinkle grated cheese over each.
5. Bake in **NuWave oven** on 5cm rack for 20 minutes until well risen. Turn out onto wire rack. Serve warm.

A delicious yet healthy alternative for breakfast or in-between snacks!

SAVORY MUFFINS

1¼ cup self raising flour
65g butter, melted
1 egg, lightly beaten
½ cup buttermilk
½ teasp paprika
2 rashers crispy bacon, chopped
½ cup grated cheese
½ cup diced tomato, seeded

1. Sift flour into bowl.
2. Add melted butter, egg, milk and paprika and mix well.
3. Add bacon, cheese and tomato; stir into mixture.
4. ¾ fill silicone muffin cups or greased muffin pan and bake in **NuWave oven** on 2cm rack, HI for 20mins. Serve warm.

Just delicious!

CHICKEN, LEEK & TARRAGON PIE

50g butter
3 tbsp plain flour
1 leek, trimmed & thinly sliced
1½ cups chicken stock
½ cup pouring cream
1 tsp dried tarragon
1 pinch white pepper
Salt to taste
1 whole cooked chicken*, deboned, meat chopped
2 sheets frozen puff pastry, thawed
1 egg, lightly whisked

1. Melt butter in a saucepan over low heat until foaming. Add leek and cook, stirring until leek softens (around 5min).
2. Add flour, stirring, for a further 3 minutes or until mixture bubbles. Remove from heat.
3. Gradually add stock, whisking until smooth. Return pan to heat and cook, stirring until mixture boils and thickens. Remove from heat.
4. Whisk cream, tarragon and pepper into the flour mixture and season with salt. Stir in chopped chicken and set aside to cool completely.
5. Pour chicken mixture into pie dish.
6. Brush edge of pie dish with egg and top pie with puff pastry. Trim edge leaving 1.5 – 2cm overhang. Brush edge with egg. Cut 3cm wide strips of pastry from extra sheet and place on top of pie around outside edge. Pinch both layers of pastry together with fingers**. Cut three slits in top pastry. With leftover pastry cut out leaves and decorate top of pie and brush whole top with egg.
7. Bake in **NuWave oven**, on 5cm rack for 30mins or until pastry is golden brown.

* A barbeque chicken can be used for this recipe, however you can cook a chicken in your **NuWave oven** just as easily and this is more cost effective!
** Join pastry by pinching. To do this, take index finger and thumb of left hand and place about 2cm from outer edge of pie, (this hand should be pointing to outside edge). Take index finger of right hand and pointing toward center of pie push outside edge of pie between the fingers of the left hand.

This pie has a delicate taste of tarragon delighting every palate!

CHICKEN, CORN & ASPARAGUS TARTS

3 sheets frozen ready-rolled puff pastry, partially thawed
2 tsp olive oil
200g chicken mince
2 green onions, thinly sliced
3 eggs
½ cup pure cream
½ x 340g bottle asparagus, drained, trimmed, cut into
1cm pieces
125g can corn kernels, drained
⅓ cup grated tasty cheese

1. Cut each pasty sheet into 4 square. Using 2 x 6-cup greased muffin pans, press 1 square into each pan hole.
2. Heat oil in a frying pan over medium-high heat. Add mince and onion; cook, stirring with a wooden spoon to break up mince, for 3-4 minutes or until mince is browned.
3. Whisk eggs and cream together in a jug. Season with pepper and salt.
4. Divide mince mixture between pan holes. Top with asparagus, corn and egg mixture. Sprinkle with cheese.
5. Bake in **NuWave oven** on 5cm rack, power level HI, for 20 mins; Carefully remove tarts from pan and place directly onto the 5cm rack and bake for a further 5 mins.

These make a delicious lunch, with salad, eat here or take away!

CHICKEN & VEGETABLE PIES

1 tbsp olive oil
30g butter
500g chicken breast filler, cut into 2cm chunks
1 leek, white part only, finely sliced
1 garlic clove, crushed
1 tbsp flour
1/3 cup white wine or water
1 cup chicken stock
½ cup thick cream
1 large carrot, peeled, cooked, diced
1 large potato, peeled, boiled, diced
1 cup frozen peas, cooked
1 tbsp chopped fresh or ½ tsp dried tarragon
4 sheets puff pastry, thawed
1 egg, lightly beaten

1. Heat olive oil and butter in a frypan over medium heat, add pieces of chicken and cook until lightly browned and almost cooked through. Transfer chicken to a plate and set aside.
2. Add leek and garlic to the pan and cook over low heat for 2-3 minutes or until softened.
3. Add the flour and cook for 1min. Add wine and bring to the boil for 1min; then pour in stock and cream and cook, stirring, for a further 5 minutes over medium-low heat.
4. Return chicken to pan with cooked vegetables and tarragon, season well, then set aside to cool.
5. Cut each pastry square into 4 squares. Place some chicken mixture in the centre of each square, then lift up the sides of the pastry to form a parcel, pinching edges together to seal. Twist top join around decoratively.

6. Place on small rounds of baking paper and brush pies with beaten egg. Bake in **NuWave oven** on 10cm rack, level 10 for 15mins; turn, and brown other side for about 5mins.

A fun and wholesome way to satisfy hungry appetites on their own or with a fresh salad!

GOUGÈRES

75g butter, chopped
1 cup water
1 cup plain flour
½ tsp salt
Pinch paprika
Tabasco to taste (I use about 6 dashes)
4 eggs
100g gruyère or gouda cheese, diced very finely

1. Combine butter, paprika, salt, Tabasco and water in saucepan, bring to the boil.
2. When butter is melted and water boiling rapidly, add sifted flour all at once: stir vigorously until mixture leaves side of saucepan and forms a smooth ball.
3. Transfer mixture to small bowl of electric mixer, add eggs one at a time, beating well after each addition. Mixture should be glossy.
4. Stir in cheese with a wooden spoon.
5. Cover 5cm rack with baking paper and drop teaspoonfuls of mixture about 5cm apart.
6. Bake in **NuWave oven**, level 10, for 15-20 minutes, turning over after 12-15mins (depending on size).
7. When timer goes off, open oven and cut a slit in side of each puff.
8. Bake in **NuWave oven**, on level 7, for a further 5 minutes to dry puffs out.
9. Can be served hot or cold.

A popular nibble with a glass of wine or make them larger and serve with a salad for lunch!

HAM & MUSHROOM QUICHE

1 sheet ready made shortcrust pastry
½ cup cream
5 eggs
½ tsp French mustard
Salt & pepper
1 cup grated cheese (your favourite cheddar will do well)
125g diced ham
125g sliced mushrooms
small head of broccoli, cut into small flowerettes

一. Grease fluted quiche pan (with removable base).
一. Line pan with pastry and trim to fit.
一. Cut baking paper big enough to overlap edges of pastry case and fill with dried beans or pasta – enough to hold pastry in shape whilst cooking*.
一. Bake in **NuWave oven** on 10cm rack, level 10 for 20 minutes, remove beans & paper, bake a further 5mins.
一. Blanch broccoli in boiling water for around 3mins.
一. Whisk eggs with mustard and salt & pepper until combined.
一. Whisk in cream.
一. Sprinkle ham, mushrooms and blanched broccoli evenly over bottom of pastry case and top with grated cheese.
一. Gently pour egg mixture over filling.
一. Bake in **NuWave oven** on 5cm rack, level 10 for 25mins. Or until filling is set.
一. Allow to cool in pan for around 10mins.
   * This is called 'blind baking' your pastry.

This quiche is delicious served warm or cold – it's great for picnics!

BAKED EGGS with SPINACH and CHERRY TOMATOES

8 eggs
150g baby spinach leaves
12 cherry tomatoes cut into halves
100g Gruyere cheese, grated
Cayenne pepper & salt

1. Blanch spinach in boiling salted water until just wilted. Drain well and squeeze out excess water.
2. Divide spinach into 4 x 1-cup greased ramekins.
3. Break 2 eggs into each ramekin and top each one with 6 cherry tomatoes halves.
4. Sprinkle with cayenne pepper and salt and top with grated cheese.
5. Bake in **NuWave oven**, on 5cm rack for 15mins or until eggs are set to your liking.

Serve with crispy bacon, chipolatas and crunchy toast fingers.

An impressive breakfast that will look like you have been up all night preparing! We won't tell!!

BREKKIE BIKKIES

1 large ripe banana (the riper the better)
¾ cup granulated sugar
¾ cup peanut butter
¼ cup water
2 egg whites
1 cup plain flour
½ cup whole wheat plain flour
½ tsp baking soda
½ tsp salt
2 cups quick-cooking rolled oats
½ cups chopped walnuts
¼ cup chocolate chips

1. In a large mixing bowl, mash banana. With electric mixer, beat in sugar, peanut butter, water and egg whites until smooth.
2. Add sifted flours, baking soda and salt.
3. Stir in remaining ingredients. Take tablespoonfuls of mixture and roll into a ball. Flatten balls with palms of hands and place on 5cm rack.
4. Bake in **NuWave oven** for 15mins, turn over and bake a further 2mins.
5. Allow to cool on wire rack.

These biscuits are a great source of fibre, protein and iron so they're just great for that member of the family who tries to dodge breakfast!

BREKKIE MUFFINS

1¼ cup self raising flour
65g butter, melted
1 egg, lightly beaten
½ cup buttermilk
½ teasp paprika
2 rashers crispy bacon, chopped
½ cup grated cheese
½ cup diced tomato, seeded

1. Sift flour into bowl.
2. Add melted butter, egg, milk and paprika and mix well.
3. Add bacon, cheese and tomato; stir into mixture.
4. ¾ fill silicone muffin cups or greased muffin pan and bake in **NuWave oven** on 2cm rack, HI for 20mins.

Serve warm.

Just delicious!

CHEESE and VEGEMITE SCROLLS

3 cups self-raising flour
Pinch salt
50g butter
375ml milk
1 - 2 tbsp vegemite
200g tasty cheese, grated
2 tbsp parmesan cheese (mix with tasty cheese)

1. Sift flour and salt into a bowl then rub through butter (alternatively, process flour & butter in food processor). Stir in enough milk to make soft dough. Knead gently on a lightly floured surface, and then roll to form a 40cm x 25cm rectangle.
2. Spread the Vegemite over the dough then sprinkle over 3/4 of the cheese. Roll up along the long side to enclose the cheese. Cut 10 x 4cm pieces from the roll and place close together, cut side up on baking paper on 5cm rack.
3. Sprinkle with the remaining cheese and bake in a **NuWave oven** for 10 minutes, turn over and bake a further 2mins.

An even faster way to prepare these is to use frozen puff pastry which has been thawed for 10mins, spread with vegemite and cheese, roll up and cook as above.
Other variations you could try include:
pizza scrolls, using cheese, capsicum and salami in a similar way
sweet chili and cheese
capsicum chutney and cheese

You could also make some pretty yummy sweet versions with chopped dried apricots, nutella or walnuts and apple pulp.

BANANA STUFFED FRENCH TOAST

1 loaf French bread (crusts removed and loaf cut into 2½cm slices)
2 bananas, peeled and sliced diagonally
3 eggs, beaten
½ cup half milk, half cream
1 tsp vanilla extract
15ml orange liqueur
zest of 1 orange
55g butter

1. Make a cut through each slice of bread leaving the bottom intact to create a pocket and fill with 3 or 4 slices of banana in each. Pack firmly in single layer into greased pan (I use a 20cm square cake tin for this).
2. In a medium bowl beat together eggs, milk/cream, vanilla extract, orange liqueur and orange zest.
3. Pour egg mixture over bread slices in pan and allow to rest for at least 30mins. (This can be done the night before and cooked the next morning)
4. Bake in **NuWave oven**, 5cm rack for 25-30mins.

Serve with yoghurt or crème fraiche.

This is just delicious for a sweet special day!

CHOCOLATE CAKE

1 cup plain flour
1 cup sugar
½ cup cocoa
1 tsp baking powder
1 tsp baking soda
½ tsp salt
1 lightly beaten egg
½ cup milk
¼ cup vegetable oil
1 tsp vanilla
½ cup boiling water
Chocolate ganache
1 punnet of fresh raspberries

—. Sift dry ingredients into a medium size mixing bowl.
—. Add egg, milk, oil and vanilla.
—. With electric mixer beat mixture on medium speed for 2-3 minutes.
—. Stir in boiling water until well combined.
—. Pour mixture into 8" x 8" (20cm x 20cm) cake pan that has been oiled and lined with baking paper.
—. Bake in **NuWave oven** on 5cm rack for 30-35 minutes.
—. Cool in pan for 10 minutes, turn out onto cooling rack and allow to cool completely.
—. Coat cake with a thin layer of chocolate ganache, place fresh raspberries evenly over top of cake and drizzle the rest of the ganache over raspberries flicking spoon from side to side turning cake to ensure even coverage.
—.

Chocolate Ganache
2/3 cup thickened cream
200g cooking chocolate

—. Place ingredients into a small saucepan.
—. Heat on medium heat until chocolate has melted and mixture is smooth.
—. Allow to cool for a few minutes and then pour gently over cake*.
—.

*Use a biscuit tray under rack to catch spill over of ganache
– this can be re-applied to cake.

*This is such a simple cake to make and is so delicious! It will be an instant winner with your family and friends! The **NuWave oven** aerates the cake during cooking and the results are in the tasting.*

EGGLESS CHOCOLATE CAKE

Ingredients
1½ cups plain flour
1 cup sugar
4 tbsp cocoa
1 teasp bicarbonate of soda
½ teasp salt
1cup water
⅓ cup vegetable oil
2 tbsp white vinegar
2 tsp vanilla extract

Method
1. Sift the dry ingredients into a bowl.
2. Combine wet ingredients and stir into flour mixture.
3. Pour mixture into greased mini muffin pans (I use my individual silicone ones); place on 5cm rack and bake in **NuWave oven** for 10 minutes (mini); 20 minutes (muffin). Cool on wire racks.

These easy little chocolate cakes are great for those allergic to egg and dairy and they taste terrific!

LEMON YOGURT SYRUP CAKE

Ingredients

250g butter, softened
3 tsp lemon rind, finely grated
¾ cup caster sugar
3 eggs
1¼ cups Greek-style yoghurt
¼ cup lemon juice
1½ cups self-raising flour
½ cup plain flour

Method

—. Grease a fluted ring pan (or Bundt pan).
—. Using an electric mixer, beat butter, lemon rind and sugar until light and fluffy.
—. Add eggs, 1 at a time, beating well after each addition.
—. Transfer mixture to a large bowl, add half the yoghurt and half the lemon juice; stir to combine; sift half the flours over butter mixture; stir to combine. Repeat with remaining yoghurt, lemon juice and flours.
—. Spread mixture into prepared pan.
—. Bake on 5cm rack in **NuWave oven**, power level HI for 45 mins or until skewer inserted in cake comes out clean. Cool in pan for 10 mins. Turn out onto a wire rack over a baking tray.
—.

Meanwhile, make lemon syrup:

—. Combine lemon juice, sugar and ¼ cup cold water in a saucepan over low heat.
—. Stir for about 5 mins or until sugar has dissolved; increase heat to medium, bring to the boil, reduce heat to low and simmer for about 5 minutes or until thickened.
—. Pour hot syrup over hot cake.

This is a beautifully textured cake with tang that is sensational served with Greek-style yoghurt and lemon zest.!

ADDITION TO RIGHT SIDE UP, UPSIDE DOWN PINEAPPLE CAKE

On page 49 of the **NuWave Recipe Book** you will find a recipe for this cake.
I prefer to use my own butter cake recipe instead of using the packaged mix. This is how I like to make it...
125g butter, chopped
2 tsp vanilla extract
¾ cup (165g) caster sugar
2 eggs
1 cup (150g) self raising flour
1 tbsp cornflour
¼ cup (60ml) milk
440g can pineapple rings
½ cup brown sugar

1. Cream butter, sugar and vanilla until light in colour.
2. Add eggs, sifted flour, cornflour and milk and beat 2–3 minutes.
3. Pour mixture into a greased 28cm pie pan.
4. Bake in **NuWave oven** on 10cm rack, level 10, for 5mins. (The top should be set enough to take the weight of the pineapple rings)
5. Lay pineapple over the top and cut some of the remaining rings to fit the gaps.
6. Sprinkle the brown sugar evenly over the top and continue cooking another 15mins.
7. Remove cake to 5cm rack and bake a further 15mins.

*The **NuWave oven** really aerates foods like cakes, potatoes, pastries etc so you find this cake is light and fluffy with a delicious gooey caramelised pineapple topping that goes perfectly with a blob of double cream or a scoop of ice cream!*

ORANGE & POLENTA SYRUP CAKE

1 cup caster sugar
3 eggs
¾ cup extra-light olive oil
1 tbsp orange rind, finely grated
¼ cup orange juice
1½ cups self-raising flour, sifted
½ cup polenta
⅓ cup almond meal (ground almonds)
2 tbsp flaked almonds

Orange Syrup

1¼ cups caster sugar
½ cup orange juice
1 cup cold water

1. Grease and line with baking paper, a 20cm spring-form pan or ring pan.
2. Whisk sugar, eggs, oil, orange rind and orange juice together in a bowl until smooth.
3. Add flour, polenta and almond meal. Stir to combine.
4. Pour into prepared pan and top with flaked almonds.
5. Bake in **NuWave oven** on 5cm rack, level 9, for 45 minutes or inserted skewer comes out clean. Cover with baking paper if over-browning during cooking. Stand in pan for 5 minutes. Turn out onto wire rack over baking tray.
6.

Make orange syrup:

1. Combine sugar, orange juice and water in a saucepan over medium heat.
2. Cook, stirring, for 2-3 minutes or until sugar has dissolved.
3. Bring to a simmer. Simmer, without stirring, for 5 minutes or until thickened.
4. Transfer to a heatproof jug.
5. Pour half of the hot syrup over hot cake.

6. Allow to stand for 15-20 minutes to slightly cool.
Serve cake with remaining syrup.

Another fantastic cake that is simple to make with exceptional results!

APPLE & CRANBERRY TURNOVERS

1 X 400g can pie apples
1/3 cup dried cranberries
4 tbsp hazelnut meal
2 tbsp caster sugar
2 sheets puff pastry
extra caster sugar
egg white

1. Mix together apples, cranberries, hazelnut meal and caster sugar until combined.
2. Cut pastry sheets into four.
3. Divide mixture between each quarter, placing mixture on one side leaving 20mm edge.
4. Brush edges of pastry with egg white, fold pastry over and seal with a fork.
5. Cut three slits in top of turnover, brush top with egg white and sprinkle with extra sugar.
6. Bake in **NuWave oven** on 10cm rack for 10 minutes, turn pastries over and cook for another 5 minutes.

Tip: Spray racks with oil or place pastries on pieces of baking paper until turned over.

Absolutely delicious served with vanilla bean ice-cream!

CINNAMON APPLE FILO PASTRIES

6 sheets filo pastry*
25g unsalted butter, melted
2 Granny Smith apples, cored, peeled, halved and thinly sliced
2 tbsp caster sugar
½ tsp cinnamon

1. Lay a sheet of filo pastry on the work surface, brush it with a little of the melted butter, then lay another sheet on top. Continue brushing with butter and layering until all six filo sheets are stacked on top of each other.
2. Using a 12cm / 4½in saucer as a guide, cut out four pastry rounds with a sharp knife.
3. Brush each pastry round with the remaining butter and place them on baking paper.
4. Arrange the apple slices on the pastry rounds, fanning them out from the centre. Dust with sugar and cinnamon.
5. Bake in the **NuWave oven** on 10cm rack, level 10 for 12 minutes, or until the pastry is golden and the apples are tender.
6. Serve with icecream or cream as desired.

Allow filo pastry to sit in packet at room temperature for 2 hours before handling – otherwise the pastry will crack and break where there are chilled bits!

CHERRY GALETTE

50g butter, softened
2 tbsp caster sugar
1 egg yolk
½ cup (60g) almond meal
1 tbsp self-raising flour
4 sheets filo pastry
30g butter, melted
200g frozen pitted cherries
2 tsp icing sugar

1. Beat softened butter, sugar and egg yolk with electric mixer 4mins or until light and fluffy. Stir in flour and almond meal.
2. Brush filo sheets with melted butter and fold in half. Stack sheets on top of each other on baking paper.
3. Spread almond mixture over pastry leaving a 4cm border.
4. Press frozen cherries into almond mixture. Fold the pastry edges in to make border.
5. Bake in **NuWave oven**, on 5cm rack, level 10, for 18mins.
6. Sprinkle with sifted icing sugar to serve. Great with ice-cream!

A quick and delicious dessert that can be made from the pantry and the freezer! Light and oh soooo tasty!

LEMON MERINGUE PIE

Biscuit Pastry
90g butter
¼ cup sugar
1 egg
1¼ cups plain flour
¼ cup self raising flour
—. Beat butter until creamy, add sugar, beat until just combined.
—. Add beaten egg gradually, beating well after each addition. (Over creaming at this stage will make pastry difficult to handle.)
—. Work in 2/3 of the sifted flours with a wooden spoon, then remaining flour with the hand.
—. Turn on to lightly floured board, knead lightly until smooth. (Heavy handling of pastry will toughen it and make it difficult to roll.)
—. Wrap in plastic wrap and refrigerate for 30min before using.
—. Roll out and line a greased 23cm fluted pie pan with removable bottom with pastry. Refrigerate for further 30 mins before baking – this helps prevent shrinkage.
—. Bake in **NuWave oven** for 15min (10cm rack); remove and allow to cool.
—.

Filling
4 tbsp plain flour
4 tbsp cornflour
2 tsp grated lemon rind
¾ cup lemon juice
1 cup sugar
1¼ cups water
90g butter
4 egg yolks
—. Combine sifted flours, lemon rind, lemon juice & sugar in saucepan. Add water, blend until smooth, stir over heat until mixture boils and thickens; this is important, the mixture must boil. Reduce heat, stir a further 2 mins.
—. Remove from heat, stir in butter and lightly beaten egg-yolks, stir until butter has melted; cool.
—. Spread cold lemon filling evenly into pastry case.

Meringue

4 egg whites
2 tbsp water
Pinch salt
¾ cup caster sugar

—. Combine egg-whites, water and salt in small bowl of electric mixer.
—. Beat on high until soft peaks form. Gradually add sugar, beat well until sugar has dissolved. (Approx 15 mins)
—. Spoon on top of lemon filling spreading meringue to edges of pie to seal; peak meringue decoratively with knife.
—. Bake in **NuWave oven** with extender ring fitted, on 5cm rack, level 8, for 15mins or until golden brown.
—.

Fantastic!!

MIXED BERRY JALOUSIE

1 cup frozen mixed berries
¼ cup (75g) caster sugar
1 sheet ready-rolled puff pastry
1 tbsp jam (your favourite - but not citrus)
1 egg white
2 tbsp caster sugar, extra

Frangipane Filling –
*(This makes enough filling for 2 jalousies – this recipe is so
delicious you will end up using it!)*
30g butter
¼ tsp vanilla extract
¼ cup caster sugar
1 egg
1 tbsp plain flour
2/3 cup (80g) almond meal

—. In a small bowl mix butter, vanilla and sugar with electric
   beater until thick and creamy.
—. Beat in egg until well combined.
—. Stir in flour and almond meal.
—.
   Make Frangipane filling.
—. Cut pastry in half lengthways and cut about 8 evenly
   spaced slits in one half making sure you don't cut through
   edges.
—. Place uncut pastry piece onto a piece of baking paper (cut
   to size) and spread with jam.
—. Place half of Frangipane filling on pastry, leaving a 2cm
   border around all sides. Cover filling with frozen mixed
   berries.
—. Brush border of pastry with egg white and place
   remaining pastry (slit piece) over the top and press edges
   together ensuring a good seal.
—. Brush jalousie with remaining egg white, sprinkle with
   extra sugar.
—. Bake in **NuWave oven**, on 10cm rack, for 20 minutes.

—. Turn jalousie over, remove baking paper and bake a further 5 minutes.
—. Serve jalousie slit side up with vanilla bean ice-cream or thick cream.
—.

This makes a delicious dessert or treat from ingredients easily found in your kitchen!

PLUM TART

125g butter
110g caster sugar
3 small eggs or 2 large eggs
¼ tsp cinnamon
½ tsp vanilla essence
Grated zest 1/3 orange
8 – 10 blood plums
100g self raising flour
25g ground almonds

1. Cream together the butter and caster sugar until light and creamy, add the eggs, beating well between each addition.
2. Fold in the flour, ground almonds, vanilla essence, orange zest and cinnamon.
3. Pour into a buttered 23cm flan tin and arrange the plum halves on top.
4. Bake in **NuWave oven** with extender ring fitted, on 5cm rack, level 10 for 35-40mins.
5. Serve with a generous scoop of vanilla bean ice-cream or a dollop of clotted cream.

The fantastic sweet friand style cake mixed with tangy plums is my favourite!

PROFITEROLES

75g butter, chopped
1 cup water
1 cup plain flour
4 eggs
—. Combine butter and water in saucepan, bring to the boil.
—. When butter is melted and water boiling rapidly, add sifted flour all at once: stir vigorously until mixture leaves side of saucepan and forms a smooth ball.
—. Transfer mixture to small bowl of electric mixer, add eggs one at a time, beating well after each addition. Mixture should be glossy.
—. Cover 5cm rack with baking paper and drop teaspoonfuls of mixture about 5cm apart.
—. Bake in **NuWave oven**, level 10, for 20 minutes, turning over after 10mins.
—. When timer goes off, open oven and cut a slit in side of each puff.
—. Bake in **NuWave oven**, on level 7, for a further 5 minutes to dry puffs out.
—. Place on cooling rack and allow to cool.
—.

When cold, fill each puff with custard/cream in a piping bag and top with chocolate sauce.

Custard Cream
2 level tbsp custard powder
1 tbsp sugar
1 cup milk
1 tsp vanilla extract
300ml carton double cream
1 tbsp icing sugar
—. Mix custard powder, sugar and enough of the milk to make a runny paste.
—. Bring milk to the boil. Remove from heat and whisk in custard paste.
—. Return to the heat and bring a simmer until thick (this custard will be thicker than normal as we are only using half the quantity of milk).
—. Remove from heat and allow to cool to room temperature.

—. Meanwhile, whip double cream with icing sugar and vanilla until thick and mix into cold custard.

Chocolate Sauce
200g dark cooking chocolate
3/4 cup cream
½ tsp vanilla extract
2 tbsp Crème de Cocao liqueur
—. Place chocolate and cream in a small saucepan and stir over a medium heat until chocolate has melted and combined.
—. Remove from heat.
—. Add vanilla and liqueur and stir until combined.

This is a delicious and popular dessert that is so easy with the NuWave you will be considered a gourmet cook!

PORTUGUESE CUSTARD TARTS

3 egg yolks
½ cup caster sugar
2 tbsp cornflour
¾ cup cream
½ cup water
strip of lemon rind
2 teasp vanilla essence
1 sheet frozen ready-rolled puff pastry

1. Grease 2 x 6-hole muffin pans.
2. Whisk egg yolks, sugar and corn-flour in medium saucepan until combined. Gradually whisk in cream and water until smooth. Add lemon rind, stir over medium heat until mixture boils and thickens.
3. Remove pan from heat, remove and discard rind, stir in vanilla essence. Cover surface of custard with plastic wrap, cool.
4. Cut pastry sheet in half. Stack the two halves on top of each other. Stand about 5mins or until thawed. Roll the pastry up tightly from the short side, then cut the log into twelve 1cm rounds. Lay pastry, cut-side up, on a floured surface, roll each round out to about 10cm (turning pastry as you go to keep round shape). Press rounds into the prepared muffin pans with your fingers.
5. Spoon cooled custard into pastry cases.
6. Bake in **NuWave oven** on 5cm rack, level 10 for 20mins. Remove tarts from pan and place directly back onto rack and bake a further 5mins.

These will be so popular you had better be prepared to make them often!

ALMOND & JAM BISCUITS

125g unsalted butter
½ cup caster sugar
1-2 tsp grated orange zest
2 eggs
1 tsp vanilla extract
pinch salt
1 cup plain flour
½ cup almond meal
1 cup slivered almonds, chopped
¾ cup raspberry or any favourite jam

Beat together butter, sugar and orange zest until light and creamy. Add eggs one at a time.
Stir through vanilla and pinch salt.
Fold through sifted flour and almond meal; knead until you get smooth, light dough.
Roll into 2 teaspoonful-sized balls and roll in the slivered almonds, pressing lightly to get them to stick to the dough. Flatten slightly and make an indentation in the middle of each biscuit and fill with jam.
Bake on baking paper on 5cm rack in **NuWave oven** (add extender ring) for 18mins.
Allow to cool 5mins on paper before transferring to cooling rack.

Delicious cakey style biscuits with a tang of orange, crunchy almonds and chewy jam centres! You will have to make double of this one!!

ARROWROOT BISCUITS (EGG-LESS)

Ingredients
⅓ cup arrowroot
1 cup plain flour/all-purpose flour
½ teasp baking powder
90g butter
¼ cup soft brown sugar
2 tbsp milk (approx.)
pinch of salt

Method
Sift the dry ingredients into a bowl, rub in the butter until the mixture is like fine breadcrumbs.
Add the sugar and milk to mix to a stiff dough.
Turn on to a floured surface and roll until very thin, prick all over with a fork and cut into approx. 5cm (2") rounds or ovals. Refrigerate dough to firm if it becomes too soft to handle.
Place on baking paper on 5cm rack and bake in **NuWave oven** for 10-15 minutes or until golden brown; turn and cook for another 5 minutes. Cool on wire racks.

TIP: Make sure baking paper is long enough to be captured by both sides of the dome when put on – this will ensure the paper does not get blown onto the biscuits by the convection during cooking!

These are delicious and although I make them for my grandson (bless him) who is allergic to egg), the whole family loves them!

BANANA BREAD

Ingredients:
5 very ripe bananas (6 if they are smaller ones)
3/4 cup white sugar
1 tsp. vanilla
2 cups plain flour
1 tsp baking powder
1 tsp baking soda
1 tsp ground cinnamon

Method:
Mash the bananas until smooth. Add sugar and vanilla and blend well.
In another bowl, mix the sifted dry ingredients until well blended and add to the bananas.
Bake in NuWave oven, on 5cm rack, power level 8, in a greased loaf pan for 45-50 minutes.

So simple: has no dairy, eggs or anything particularly allergenic. I've tried using gluten free flour, and that works too!

RASPBERRY & COCONUT SLICE

1 cup plain flour
65g butter, chopped coarsely
1 egg yolk
2 tbsp water, approximately
¼ cup raspberry jam
1 cup desiccated coconut
1 egg, beaten lightly
¼ cup caster sugar

Place flour in a medium bowl; rub in butter using fingertips. Add egg yolk and enough of the water to make a firm dough when ingredients are pressed together using hands.

Turn dough onto a lightly floured surface, knead gently until smooth. Place dough into a 20cm x 20cm greased pan. Use a glass to roll dough evenly over base of pan (or use fingertips).

Bake in **NuWave oven**, on 5cm rack, for 20mins or until browned lightly; stand for 10min.

Spread jam evenly over pastry.

Combine coconut, egg and sugar in medium bowl; mix using fork until all the coconut is moist. Spread coconut mixture over jam; do not flatten.

Bake in **NuWave oven** on 5cm rack for 8 minutes until golden brown. Allow to cool in pan. Cut into squares.

An old favourite that still wins hearts!

SCONES

21/2 cups self raising flour
1 tsp salt
¼ cup cream
1 tsp vanilla extract
1 cup lemonade (fresh)

Sift flour and salt into a medium bowl.
Make well in center of flour and add cream, vanilla & lemonade.
Cut through mixture with a knife until mixed.
Turn out sticky dough mixture onto lightly floured bench or pastry sheet, sprinkle lightly with flour and gently knead dough until smooth.
Pat down to about 3cm (1") high and cut scones with a 5cm (2") round cutter.
Lightly spray bottom of pan (that comes with your extender kit) or a small flat tray with spray oil.
Place scones in pan about 1cm-2cm apart and brush tops with milk.
Bake in **NuWave oven** on 5cm rack (that comes with your extender kit) for 10-12 mins on level 10 – there is no need to set this level as your **NuWave** will default to this setting automatically. I like to turn my scones over for the last 2 minutes but this is not necessary!
Remove from oven and allow to cool on rack.

Serve with your favourite jam and cream!

MACADAMIA & GINGER ANZAC BISCUITS

125g butter
2 tbsp golden syrup
½ tsp bicarbonate of soda
2 tbsp boiling water
1 cup (90g) rolled oats
1cup (150g) plain flour
1 cup (220g) firmly packed brown sugar
¾ cup (60g) desiccated coconut
½ cup (65g) finely chopped macadamias
¼ cup (45g) finely chopped glace ginger

Combine oats, flour, sugar, coconut, macadamias and ginger in a large bowl.

Mix butter and golden syrup in a small saucepan over a low heat until smooth.

Stir in combined bi-carb soda and water and pour mixture over dry ingredients.

Roll level tablespoons of mixture into balls, slightly flatten with a fork when placing on a piece of baking paper (about 5cm apart) on 5cm rack of **NuWave oven**.

Bake on power level 8 for 15 minutes.

Cool on cooling rack.

These are my favourite Anzac biscuits - enjoy!

EASY TWO-EGG PAVLOVA

2 egg-whites
1½ cups caster sugar
½ teasp vanilla
1 teasp vinegar
1 teasp cornflour
4 tbsp boiling water

Method

Place all ingredients into small bowl of electric mixer, beat on high speed until mixture is very stiff (approx 15min).

Spread onto prepared baking paper on 5cm rack.

Bake in **NuWave oven**, power level 8, with extender ring added, for 40 minutes.

Allow to cool in oven with dome propped open about 1cm (I use a spoon to do this).

This is a delicious crispy meringue, slightly chewy and just such a treat when filled with fresh whipped cream and fresh seasonal fruits!

CLASSIC PAVLOVA

5 egg whites
1¼ cups caster sugar
1½ tsp vanilla
1½ tsp white vinegar
1½ tbsp corn flour
Pinch salt

Beat egg whites until stiff.
Add caster sugar slowly and then salt.
Beat for a further 5 minutes until thick, stiff peaks form.
Beat in vanilla and vinegar, then fold in corn flour.
Spoon mixture onto baking paper with a 20cm circle drawn onto it and pile meringue high.
Bake in **NuWave oven,** with extender ring attached on 5cm rack, level 6 for 35 minutes.
Allow to cool in oven by propping open the dome about 2cm.
Top with whipped cream, fresh strawberries, kiwi fruit, sliced banana and passion fruit.

This is a beautiful meringue that is marshmallowy in the middle and crispy on the outside!

APPLE SPONGE PUDDING

8 Granny Smith apples, peeled & cored (4 apples chopped
and 2 thinly sliced)
½ cup caster sugar
1 tsp grated lemon rind
¼ cup water
2 eggs
⅓ cup caster sugar, extra
2 tbsp cornflour
2 tbsp plain flour
2 tbsp self-raising flour

Combine apples, sugar, rind and water in saucepan, bring
to boil, reduce heat, simmer, covered, for about 15
minutes or until tender.
Pour hot apple mixture into a deep, greased, ovenproof
dish (6 cup capacity).
Beat eggs in a small bowl with electric mixer until thick
and creamy.
Gradually add extra sugar, beating until dissolved between
each addition.
Sift flours over egg mixture and fold through gently.
Spread mixture evenly over hot apple mixture.
Bake in **NuWave oven** on 5cm rack, level 10 for 20-
25mins.

*Sensational served with custard, cream or ice-cream! A nice
alternative is to replace 6 of the apples with chopped rhubarb. You
will need about 425g or 5 cups rhubarb.*

BAKED RICE PUDDINGS

2 cups milk
300ml thin cream
½ cup medium grain (calrose) rice, rinsed, drained
½ cup caster sugar
1 cinnamon stick
1 vanilla bean, split, seeds scraped
Pinch ground nutmeg, plus extra to sprinkle
2 strips lemon rind
2 egg yolks

Method

Combine milk, cream, rice, sugar, cinnamon, vanilla
bean and seeds, nutmeg and lemon rind in a medium
saucepan. Cook over medium heat, stirring
occasionally, for 5 minutes or until it reaches a simmer.
Remove from heat and set aside for 15 minutes to
infuse.
Put rice mixture through a sieve. Remove and discard
the cinnamon stick, lemon rind and vanilla bean.
Equally divide rice into casserole dishes.
Add egg yolks to milk mixture and whisk to combine.
Pour milk mixture equally into 4 x 1-cup casserole
dishes over rice.
Bake in **NuWave oven** with extender ring fitted, power
level 10, on 5cm rack for 10mins. Stir and sprinkle with
extra nutmeg; bake a further 30mins or until rice is
tender and custard is set.
Remove from oven and allow to stand for 10 minutes
before serving.
Serve warm with stewed fruit.

*Another family favourite cooked to perfection in the **NuWave** oven!*

BANANA PUDDINGS

90g butter, melted
½ cup almond meal
3 egg whites
¾ cup icing sugar
¼ cup plain flour
25g butter, melted, extra
2 tbsp brown sugar, firmly packed 2 medium bananas,
sliced thickly

Grease four 9.5cm-round 2/3 cup (160ml) ovenproof
dishes (I use pie dishes for this).
Combine butter, almond meal, egg whites, icing sugar
and flour in medium bowl; stir until just combined.
Divide extra butter equally among prepared dishes;
sprinkle evenly with brown sugar. Divide banana slices
and then pudding mixture equally among dishes.
Bake in **NuWave oven** on 5cm rack for 15mins.
When cooked stand puddings 2mins, then run knife
around edge and turn out onto serving plates.
Serve with custard, cream or icecream.

*This has to be one of the easiest desserts to make but the results will
surprise everyone! Delicious!*

BREAD & BUTTER PUDDING

6 thin slices white bread, crust removed
40g butter
3 eggs
¼ cup caster sugar
2 cups milk
1 teasp vanilla essence
½ cup sultanas
Nutmeg or cinnamon

Method

Sprinkle sultanas over base of extender dish.
Butter bread and cut into triangles. Arrange in bottom of extender dish (single layer but overlapping slightly) butter side up.
Whisk eggs, sugar, milk and essence together in bowl. Pour half the custard mixture over bread, stand for 10 minutes.
Whisk remaining egg mixture again; pour into dish.
Sprinkle with nutmeg or cinnamon.
Place on 5cm rack and bake in **NuWave oven**, power level 8, for 30 minutes, or until custard is set.

This family favourite is so popular and easy when done in the NuWave!

CARAMEL, BOURBON PUDDING

2 stale croissants
100g caster sugar
2 tbsp water
125ml double cream
125ml full-fat milk
2 tbsp bourbon
2 eggs, beaten

Tear croissants into pieces and put in a small gratin dish (about 500ml capacity).
Place caster sugar and water in a saucepan, swirl around to help dissolve sugar before putting pan on medium – high heat.
Caramelise the sugar and water mixture by letting it bubble away, without stirring, until it all turns a deep amber colour – this will take around 3-5 minutes. Keep looking but don't be too timid!
Turn down heat to low. Add cream, whisking away, milk and bourbon.
Take off the heat and still whisking, add beaten eggs.
Pour custard over croissants and leave to steep for 10 minutes.
Bake in **NuWave oven** on 5cm rack, level 10 for 10 minutes, add extender ring and bake a further 10 minutes

This is a dessert that will surprise everyone – the bourbon gives the custard a fantastic flavour!

EASTER HOT CROSS BUN PUDDING

6 hot cross buns
¼ cup white choc bits
1cup milk
1cup thin cream
5 eggs
¼ cup caster sugar
½ tsp vanilla extract
¼ cup dark choc bits
¼ cup slivered almonds

Grease a 22cm pie-dish (or shallow casserole dish) and line bottom with baking paper.
Slice hot cross buns into six slices, discarding the dark ends.
Using half of the slices, line base of tin fitting them in snugly.
Sprinkle over the white choc bits.
Whisk eggs, milk, cream, sugar and vanilla together in a large jug.
Pour half the mixture over buns.
Top with remaining slices, pour over rest of egg mixture.
Allow to stand for 30 mins.
Top with dark choc bits and slivered almonds and bake in **NuWave oven**, 5cm rack, level 8 for 50-55 mins until set and brown (it will rise when cooked and drop down on cooling).
Cool completely in tin. Run knife around edge of pudding and turn onto plate. Remove paper and invert pudding onto serving plate.
Cut into wedges to serve.

A sweet, elegant dessert that will please palates of all ages!

BAKED FILLED PEACH HALVES

6 slip-stone peaches, halved with stone removed
¼ cup sultanas
¼ cup slivered almonds
2 almond macaroons, crushed
2 tbsp brown sugar
¼ cup honey

Mix together sultanas, slivered almonds, macaroons and brown sugar until combined.
Fill each peach half with mixture, piling it as high as it will hold and dividing the mixture evenly among the peaches.
Drizzle honey over the topping of each peach until filling is well coated.
Bake in **NuWave oven**, on 5cm rack for 15mins or until peaches are cooked through (test with skewer).
Serve with custard, double cream or ice-cream and sprinkled with additional crushed macaroons.

These are fabulous and are just perfect for any occasion from the kids' after dinner treat to a perfect dessert to top off a dinner party!

FRUIT KEBABS WITH PASSIONFRUIT & ORANGE SAUCE

½ cup water
¼ cup orange juice
½ cup caster sugar
1 tbsp honey
½ cup passionfruit pulp
2 tbsp orange flavoured liqueur, optional
1 small pineapple, chopped coarsely
1 small pawpaw, chopped coarsely
2 large bananas, sliced thickly
250g strawberries
You will need about six passionfruit for this recipe or canned passionfruit pulp works just as well.
Cointreau or Grand Marnier makes the sauce exquisite!

To make sauce, combine water, juice, sugar and honey in a small saucepan.

Stir over heat, without boiling, until sugar dissolves; then bring to the boil. Reduce heat; simmer, without stirring, about 10 minutes or until mixture thickens slightly.

Remove from heat, stir in passionfruit pulp and liqueur, cool sauce 5 minutes.

Meanwhile, thread fruit onto skewers and brush with passionfruit sauce.

Place kebabs in **NuWave oven** on 10cm rack and balance of passionfruit sauce in ovenproof dish on liner tray and cook for 8 minutes.

Serve kebabs drizzled with warm passionfruit/orange sauce and icecream.

*Enjoy another fantastic treat sensation from your **NuWave oven**!*

PLUM CRUMBLES

40g butter, chopped
¼ cup self raising flour
2 tbsp brown sugar
⅓ cup rolled oats
¼ cup macadamia nuts, chopped
825g can whole plums, drained, halved, stones removed
1 cup vanilla yoghurt
½ tsp mixed spice

Combine flour and sugar in a medium bowl. Add butter.
Using fingertips, rub butter into flour mixture until
mixture resembles breadcrumbs.
Stir in oats and macadamias.
Divide plums between 4 x greased ramekins (1 cup
capacity). Sprinkle flour mixture over plums.
Stir in cheese with a wooden spoon.
Bake in **NuWave oven** on 5cm rack, level 10, for 15
minutes, until plums are hot and top is golden. Meanwhile,
combine yoghurt and mixed spice in a bowl.

Serve crumble with spiced yoghurt.

Such an easy dessert to make and the ingredients can be kept on hand!

QUEEN PUDDINGS

2 cups (140g) stale breadrumbs
1 tbsp caster sugar
1tsp vanilla extract
1 tsp finely grated lemon rind
2½ cups (625ml) milk
60g butter
4 eggs, separated
¼ cup (80g) raspberry jam, warmed
¾ cup (165g) castor sugar, extra
Grease 6 x ¾ cup (180ml) ovenproof ramekins.

Combine breadcrumbs, sugar, vanilla and rind in a large bowl.
Heat milk and butter in a medium saucepan until almost boiling, pour over bread mixture, stand 10 minutes.
Stir in yolks.
Divide mixture among ramekins.
Bake in **NuWave oven**, on 5cm rack, level 10, for 20mins.
Gently spread tops of puddings with warm jam.
Beat egg whites in a small bowl with electric mixer until soft peaks form, gradually add extra sugar, beating until sugar dissolves.
Spoon meringue over puddings and bake in **NuWave oven**, 5cm rack, extender ring added for a further 10mins.

A sweet, elegant dessert that will please palates of all ages!

HUMMINGBIRD MUFFINS w CREAMED HONEY SPREAD

1¼ self raising flour
½ tsp cinnamon
½ cup caster sugar
1 egg, lightly beaten
¼ cup olive oil
½ cup walnuts, chopped
1 ripe banana, mashed
220g can crushed pineapple in juice
1 small can of pineapple pieces (for decoration only)

Sift flour and cinnamon into a large bowl and stir in sugar. Add egg, oil, walnuts, banana and pineapple and stir until mixture is just combined.

Spoon mixture into greased 6-hole muffin pan or silicone individual muffin pans to 2/3 of the way up the sides. Top each muffin with a piece of pineapple.

Bake in **NuWave oven** on 5cm rack, level 10 for 20mins; allow to cool in pan/s.

When cold, dust muffins with icing sugar and serve with a generous dollop of Creamed Honey Spread.

Creamed Honey Spread
250g light cream cheese, chopped
2 tbsp icing sugar
¼ cup creamed honey
Place all ingredients into a bowl and beat with a spoon until smooth. Refrigerate.

My family love these muffins and the creamed honey spread makes them even more special! Enjoy!

RASPBERRY & COCONUT MUFFINS

2½ cups self raising flour
90g butter, chopped
1 cup caster sugar
1¼ cups buttermilk
1 egg, lightly beaten
1/3 cup desiccated coconut
150g fresh or frozen raspberries
2 tbsp shredded coconut

Place flour in a large bowl, rub in butter (alternatively, process flour & butter in food processor).

Stir in sugar, buttermilk, egg, desiccated coconut and raspberries until just combined – do not over-mix!

Divide mixture among holes of 2 greased 6 hole muffin pans or 12 silicone muffins holders and sprinkle with shredded coconut.

Bake in **NuWave oven**, 5cm rack for 15-18mins or until muffin springs back when lightly pressed.

Stand muffins in pan for 5mins before turning out onto wire rack to cool.

The tang of the raspberries and the sweetness of the coconut are a match made in heaven!

BACON & CORN PIZZA

1 large round pita bread
1 tbsp corn relish
1 rasher rindless bacon, finely chopped
¼ cup grated pizza cheese (a mixture of mozzarella, parmesan & tasty cheese)
1 tbsp fresh flat-leaf parsley, coarsely chopped

Spread pita bread with relish. Top with bacon and cheese.
Cook in **NuWave Oven**, on 10cm rack, for 10mins.
Sprinkle with parsley just before serving.

So quick and easy the kids (big and little) can make their own!

PIZZA

Large rounds of pita bread
Tomato sauce (use your own recipe or the bottled variety for spaghetti is easily found at your supermarket)
1 cup of pizza cheese (this is a mixture of mozzarella, parmesan, cheddar)
Choice of toppings

一. Bake pita bread in **NuWave oven** on 10cm rack for 3mins.
一. Remove from oven and turn bread over – lightly spread this side with tomato sauce.
一. Add your choice of toppings, sprinkle with cheese.
一. Bake in **NuWave oven** on 10cm rack for 8mins
一.

Suggested Toppings:

Cabanossi, pepperoni, salami or ham with
Mushrooms, capsicum, spanish onion, pineapple, olives, capers, anchovies
Fresh tomato, bocconcini, fresh basil
Prawns

These mouth-watering pizzas are not only easy to make but much more nutritious than the ones you buy!

CHILI CON CARNE PINWHEELS

500g beef mince
210g can red kidney beans, drained
35g pkt taco seasoning mix (use half for less spicy)
¼ cup fresh parsley, finely chopped
1 tbsp tomato paste
1 egg, lightly whisked
Salt & pepper to taste
2 sheets puff pastry, thawed
½ cup baby spinach leaves
¼ cup grated tasty cheese
1 egg, whisked (for egg wash)
Sour cream to serve

Place mince, beans, seasoning mix, parsley, tomato paste and egg in a large bowl. Season with salt and pepper. Using your hands, mix until well combined. Divide mixture into two equal portions. Spread each pastry sheet with a portion of beef mixture, leaving 2cm border around edges. Top meat on each sheet with half of the spinach leaves and half of the cheese. Roll pastry lengthways to enclose filling.
Place seam-side down on chopping board, brush with egg wash and gently cut each roll into 2cm-thick slices. Place slices onto baking paper on 10cm rack.
Bake in **NuWave oven** on 10cm rack, level 10 for 15mins, turn and cook a further 5mins.
Serve warm with sour cream.

These can be made ahead (before cutting) and refrigerated or frozen until ready for use!
Delicious!

CRUNCHY SAUSAGE ROLLS

1 sheet puff pastry
250g beef mince
1 stick celery, very finely chopped
½ tsp Worcestershire sauce
1 tsp tomato sauce
1 tsp cornflour
1 egg, lightly beaten (for egg wash)

Mix mince, celery, sauces and cornflour together.
Cut pastry into 16 squares (4 down and 4 across).
Shape teaspoons of meat mixture into balls and roll
into 5cm sausages. Place diagonally onto pastry square
and pinch other corners together.
Brush each sausage roll with egg wash. Cover 10cm
rack with a piece of baking paper and place rolls onto
paper.
Bake in **NuWave oven** (level 10), 10cm rack, for 15
minutes, turning over for last 5 minutes.

These are fantastic for a quick snack for the kids or when entertaining they go great with a drink!

CURRY PUFFS

400g beef mince ¼ cup tomato sauce (I use spaghetti sauce)
30g butter ½ cup water
1 clove garlic 1 tbsp fruit chutney
1 large onion, chopped Salt and Pepper
¼ tsp chili powder 1 Egg yolk
½ tsp ground ginger 1 tbsp water, extra
½ tsp turmeric 3-4 sheets puff pastry, thawed
2 tsp curry powder
½ tsp paprika

Heat butter in pan, add meat, onion and crushed garlic.
Cook, stirring, until meat is golden brown, pushing
meat with fork so that there are no hard lumps; pour
off any surplus fat.
Add chili powder, ginger, turmeric, paprika, curry
powder, tomato sauce, water, and fruit chutney.
Season with salt and pepper; mix well. Simmer gently,
uncovered, for 15mins or until mixture is very thick.
Cool completely.
Cut pastry sheets into 8cm rounds with pastry cutter.
Brush each round with combined egg-yolk and extra
water.
Place a teaspoonful of mixture on each round; fold to
form a half-circle. Press edges together firmly. Brush
tops with egg mixture.
Bake in **NuWave oven** on 10cm rack, level 10 for
10mins; turn and cook a further 4mins or until pastry
is puffed and golden brown.

This recipe is a must for entertainers! It's a real winner!

HAM and EGG TARTS

6 slices bread
6 eggs
200g shaved ham, chopped
6 cherry tomatoes, halved
¼ cup grated tasty cheese
1 tbsp chopped parsley
Spray oil
Pepper & Salt

Using a rolling pin, flatten bread slices; spray both sides with oil.
Line 6-hole muffin pan with flattened bread and crack an egg into each one.
Top eggs with chopped ham, cherry tomatoes, cheese and salt & pepper.
Bake in **NuWave oven** on 5cm rack, level 10 for 10min. Remove from pan and place directly onto rack and bake a further 8mins.

These make an excellent breakfast on the run, cold in lunch boxes or fabulous for a picnic

MEXICAN BAGELS

1 bagel
1 tbsp bottled tomato salsa
½ small avocado, sliced thickly
2 slices cheddar cheese

Split bagel in half horizontally.
Spread 2 teaspoons of salsa over each bagel half.
Top each half with avocado and one cheese slice.

Cook in **NuWave oven**, on 10cm rack, for 5mins.
For 2 or more bagels, increase the ingredients accordingly.

Nothing cooks bagels better than the NuWave Oven!

PESTO STARS

30g butter, softened
2 sheets puff pastry, thawed
2 tbsp pesto (this can be basil, sun dried tomato or your favourite)
½ cup parmesan cheese, finely grated

Combine pesto and butter in a small bowl.
Spread pesto mixture over pastry sheets, sprinkle with cheese.
Using a star shaped pastry cutter, cut stars from pasty sheets, place onto baking paper or well oiled 10cm rack.
Bake in **NuWave oven** on 10cm rack, level 10 for 5mins; turning for last minute if you wish.

A festive look with a festive flavour to have with a drink!

PITA CRISPS

Pita bread
Olive oil
Sea salt flakes (easily obtained from good supermarkets)
一. Brush oil over both sides of the bread.
一. Sprinkle top-side with salt flakes and cut into wedges.
一. Bake in **Nu-Wave oven** on 10cm rack for 5 minutes.
一.

*A great snack to serve when having a drink or a much
better alternative to potato crisps. To add some difference
you may like to add some crushed garlic to the oil or
sprinkle your favourite spice mix instead of the salt.*

Try them – they're a winner!

BIANCA'S BUTTER BISCUITS

From: Bianca 13 years old, Melbourne

Ingredients:
* 175 soft unsalted butter * 1 teaspoon baking powder
* 200g caster sugar * 1 teaspoon salt
* 2 large eggs * 300g icing sugar, sieved and food
* 400g plain flour (plus more if needed) colouring

Required:
Biscuit cutters
2 baking sheets greased or lined

1. Cream the butter and sugar together until pale and moving towards mousiness, then beat in the eggs and vanilla.
2. In another bowl, combine the flour, baking powder and salt. Add the dry ingredients to the butter and egg. Mix gently but surely. If the mixture is too sticky to be rolled out, add more flour but do so sparingly as too much will make the dough tough.
3. Halve the dough, make them into fat discs, wrap each half in clingwrap and rest in the fridge for a least 1hour.
4. Sprinkle a suitable surface with flour, place a disc of dough on it (don't take the other half out of the fridge until finished with the first). Sprinkle a little more flour on top of the disc.
5. Roll it out to a thickness of about 1/2cm.
6. Cut into shape, (dipping the cutter into flour as you go) place the biscuits a little apart on the baking sheets.
7. Bake in **NuWave oven** on 5cm rack, for 8-10 minutes, by which time they will be lightly golden around the edges.
8. Cool on a rack and continue with the remaining dough.
9. When they are completely cooled, you can get on with the icing.
10. Put a couple of tablespoons of almost boiling water into a large bowl. Add the sieved icing sugar and mix together, adding more water as you need to form a thick paste. Colour and decorate as desired.

Makes 50-60

HOMMUS

200g chick peas, drained
¼ cup vegetable stock
2 cloves garlic
2 tbsp lemon juice
2 tbsp tahini

1. Place everything in the tall cup fitted with the cross-blade.
2. Blend until smooth.

Serve with pita crisps baked in your NuWave!

CAPSICUM & CASHEW PESTO

¾ cup red capsicum, roasted in NuWave oven, skin removed
⅓ cup dry-roasted cashew nuts
2 cloves garlic, chopped
2 tbsp fresh oregano leaves
2 tbsp olive oil
⅓ cup parmesan cheese, finely grated

1. Place all ingredients, except parmesan cheese, into large cup of **NuWave Twister.**
2. Process by pulsating (turning on and off in spurts), scraping down sides as needed, until smooth.
3. Transfer to a bowl, add parmesan, season with salt and pepper and stir to combine.

Delicious served with Pita Crisps!

PESTO

1 bunch (80g) fresh basil leaves
25g pine nuts
1 large clove garlic
65g parmesan cheese
100ml extra virgin olive oil

1. Toast pine nuts by placing them in the extender kit pan and bake in **NuWave oven** on 10cm rack for 4mins.
2. Place the basil, pine nuts, garlic and parmesan in the tall cup of the **Twister** with half of the oil.
3. Fitted with cross blade, blend for a couple of minutes; add the balance of the oil and continue to blend until mixture is smooth.

Delicious with pasta for lunch or dinner or just enjoy it as a dip with fresh vegetable sticks!

CPSIA information can be obtained at www.ICGtesting.com
Printed in the USA
LVOW05s1147020115

421072LV00003B/233/P

9 781936 828258